W9-DGB-452

Here is your registration code to access
McGraw-Hill's *Folio*Live

certiorari-91183471

This code gives you access to the Instructor Web resources for *Folio*Live. Once the code is entered, you will have access to *Folio*Live for 45 days. If you choose to adopt FolioLive for your course, contact your local McGraw-Hill Representative to receive a desk passcode for extended access.

▶ REGISTERING FOR *FOLIO*LIVE

To gain access to your *Folio*Live site and resources, complete the following steps:

1. Use your Web browser to go to: **www.foliolive.com**
2. Click on "Instructors - Click here to REGISTER"
3. Enter the Registration Code* that is printed on this form.
4. After you have entered your registration code, click on **REGISTRATION**.
5. Follow the instructions to set-up your personal UserID and Password.
6. Write your UserID and Password in the space provided in your User Guide to *Folio*Live.

Thank you, and welcome to McGraw-Hill's *Folio*Live.

The **McGraw·Hill** Companies

ISBN 0-07-288702-8

INSTRUCTOR'S GUIDE TO FOLIOLIVE

Boston   Burr Ridge, IL   Dubuque, IA   Madison, WI   New York
San Francisco   St. Louis   Bangkok   Bogotá   Caracas   Kuala Lumpur
Lisbon   London   Madrid   Mexico City   Milan   Montreal   New Delhi
Santiago   Seoul   Singapore   Sydney   Taipei   Toronto

INSTRUCTOR'S GUIDE TO FOLIOLIVE

Published by McGraw-Hill Higher Education, an imprint of The McGraw-Hill Companies, Inc., 1221 Avenue of the Americas, New York, NY 10020.

1 2 3 4 5 6 7 8 9 0 TCG 0 3 2 1

ISBN 0-07-288702-8

www.mhhe.com

TABLE OF CONTENTS

How to Order *Folio*Live v

Preface vii

An Overview of *Folio*Live 1

How To Use *Folio*Live 3
Introduction 4
Logging-in and Creating Your Account 7
Creating Your Homepage 8
Creating Course Web Pages 12
Creating Custom Designs 17
Creating Frameworks 21
Using *Manage Files* 26
Registering and Managing Students 28
Providing Feedback on Student Portfolios 31
Getting Help 34

Appendix: *User's Guide to* Folio*Live* 35

Glossary G-1

Index I-1

HOW TO ORDER *Folio*LIVE

To order *Folio*Live for a course, provide your bookstore with the ISBN 0-07-283582-6 when you submit your book order. By purchasing *Folio*Live, your students will receive a *User Guide for* Folio*Live* and a passcode that will allow them access to *Folio*Live for one year. Students can renew their access in one-year increments online through their *Folio*Live accounts. Students may also purchase access to FolioLive at **www.foliolive.com**.

To request an instructor's desk passcode (available upon adoption of *Folio*Live), contact your local McGraw-Hill representative. To find your local representative, go to www.mhhe.com and click "Rep Locator." Your desk passcode allows you extended access to *Folio*Live.

PREFACE

INTRODUCING *FOLIO*LIVE

Increasingly, pre-service teachers are building portfolios in teacher training programs and continuing to develop them throughout their teaching careers. As technology becomes an integral part of education, a logical progression has been to make portfolios available electronically. "More and more institutions are encouraging – or even requiring – students to create 'electronic portfolios' that highlight their academic work and help them reflect on their campus experiences." This quotation begins Jeffrey R. Young's article "Creating Online Portfolios Can Help Students See 'Big Picture,' Colleges Say," published in the February 21, 2002 edition of *The Chronicle of Higher Education*. This article provided an impetus for the creation of *Folio*Live. Instructors in numerous schools of education have wanted to use electronic portfolios in their courses, but have found obstacles such as insufficient technical knowledge, limited school resources, and a lack of time to invest in creating and supporting an e-portfolio system kept them from doing so. *Folio*Live answers the needs of these instructors and universities, and their students, by providing an easy way to create, evaluate, and maintain electronic portfolios.

THE STORY OF *FOLIO*LIVE: THE PEOPLE

McGraw-Hill began the development of *Folio*Live by posing a series of questions to several instructors already using electronic portfolios in their courses. These instructors were asked what capabilities they wanted in an electronic portfolio tool and what features would be most beneficial to have in such a tool. They answered that they wanted an electronic portfolio tool that allowed students to:

- Upload any type of file
- Organize artifacts around standards
- Have multiple portfolios to meet the needs of different situations
- Add introductions and/or reflections to each artifact

The tool should:

- Be easy to use
- Have a Help Desk to answer students' technical questions
- Be affordably priced (the approximate cost of a brief textbook)
- Be available online, but allow students to download their portfolios and brief burn them onto a CD-Rom
- Allow the instructor to provide feedback directly to each student
- Have a user guide

Using the feedback provided by this group of expert instructors, McGraw-Hill created a preliminary version of *Folio*Live which was then reviewed by a larger group of instructors. This second review produced a wealth of feedback that helped finalize *Folio*Live. Professors who participated in demonstrations of *Folio*Live at the annual meeting of the American Educational Research Association (AERA) in April 2002 in turn provided additional feedback on how *Folio*Live could be revised to meet their needs.

McGraw-Hill would like to take this opportunity to acknowledge the instructors who provided valuable guidance and feedback during the development of *Folio*Live:

Kerri Johnson, *University of Washington*
Natalie B. Milman, *George Washington University*
Cris E. Guenter, *California State University, Chico*
Diane E. Newby, *Central Michigan University*
Mary Elizabeth Hrabe, *University of Virginia*
Tricia Ryan, *Towson University*
Jerry P. Galloway, *Indiana University Northwest*
Joyce Morris, *University of Vermont*
Kristie Walsdorf, *Florida State University*
Iris D. Johnson, *Miami University*
Brenda Frieden, *Pittsburg State University*
Lori A. Norton-Meier, *Kansas State University*
Vickie Williams, *University of Maryland Baltimore County*
V. Vanese Delahoussaye, *Houston Community College*
Paul Walsh, *Johns Hopkins University*
Leslie J. Davison, *St. Cloud State University*
Saundra L. Wetig, *University of Nebraska at Omaha*
Frank Guldbrandsen, *University of Minnesota*

THE STORY OF *FolioLive*: THE TECHNOLOGY

A key goal of McGraw-Hill Higher Education's mission is to provide quality content and technology-enhanced delivery of instructional content and services. As a leading college publisher, McGraw-Hill has dedicated vast resources to producing technology products and instructor support materials which align both students and instructors with the technological demands of today's classrooms and their future work environment. McGraw-Hill is dedicated to providing technology products such as *Folio*Live that support instructors and allow students to expand their learning.

*Folio*Live is based on the proven technology of McGraw-Hill's highly successful PageOut course management product. Launched in 1999, PageOut is currently used by over 60,000 instructors.

BENEFITS TO THE INSTRUCTOR

*Folio*Live was developed to be used in the college classroom. It was developed with both students *and* instructors in mind. Key features for the instructor include:

- **Instructor's area.** The *Folio*Live instructor's area allows instructors to create customized *Folio*Live course Web pages ensuring that student portfolios match the goals of their courses.
- **Instructors can provide direct feedback to students.** Using the *Folio*Live instructor's area, instructors can provide direct feedback on student portfolios (see *Providing Feedback on Student Portfolios* on page 31).
- ***Folio*Live is easy to order.** Order *Folio*Live through your bookstore the way you would order any class text using ISBN 0-07-283582-6. See *How to Order **Folio**Live* on page v for more information.
- **There is no cost to your school.** Students purchase *Folio*Live the same way they would purchase a class text, at no cost to the school. Student portfolios and instructor course Web pages sit on a McGraw-Hill server. Initial access to *Folio*Live for one year costs the same as a brief, softcover text. Upon adoption of *Folio*Live, instructors receive complimentary access.
- **There are no special technical requirements.** Students and instructors can access *Folio*Live through the Internet using a PC or Mac.
- ***Folio*Live is supported by a McGraw-Hill Help Desk.** The McGraw-Hill Help Desk is available to help instructors with lost passwords and technical questions.

BENEFITS TO THE STUDENT

*Folio*Live allows students to easily create professional-looking electronic portfolios. The student can:

- **Create an electronic portfolio in a few simple steps.** The student creates a portfolio by choosing to create a custom or Framework portfolio, selecting a design, and then adding artifacts (uploading existing files or creating new artifacts using a *Folio*Live template).

- **Easily organize portfolios around standards.** *Folio*Live standards-based Frameworks based on key standards (such as INTASC, NBPTS, and ISTE) allow the easy construction of portfolios based on standards.
- **Create multiple electronic portfolios.** Students can construct several portfolios to meet the needs of different situations. For example, a student might have a course portfolio, an INTASC portfolio, and an interview portfolio.
- **Add introductions and/or reflections to each artifact.** Students can add introductions and/or reflections to each artifact to demonstrate growth and reflection.
- **Download their portfolios.** Students can download their portfolios onto their local systems to burn onto a CD-ROM.
- **Get support from a McGraw-Hill Help Desk.** The McGraw-Hill Help desk is available to help students with lost passwords and technical questions.

YOUR INVOLVEMENT WITH *FOLIO*LIVE

Classroom instructors have already played an important role in the development of *Folio*Live. We now invite *you* to become involved with *Folio*Live. Let us know how well *Folio*Live meets your needs. What capabilities would you add? Email us your feedback at **education@mcgraw-hill.com**.

AN OVERVIEW OF *FolioLive*

The instructor's area of *Folio*Live was created to allow easy integration of *Folio*Live into college courses. Through the *Folio*Live instructor's area, the instructor can:

- Create a Homepage
- Create individual Course Web Pages that link to student portfolios
- Create Frameworks (portfolio tables of contents) for their students to access
- Provide direct feedback on student portfolios
- Receive support from the McGraw-Hill Help Desk

The student's area of *Folio*Live was created to allow users to easily create a professional-looking electronic portfolio. Through *Folio*Live's student area, the student can:

- Create a Homepage
- Create a professional-looking electronic portfolio
- Create a custom portfolio or use a *Folio*Live Framework
- Easily organize a portfolio around standards by using a *Folio*Live Framework or by creating a custom portfolio
- Upload any type of file (from Word to PowerPoint to audio to video) to be used as an artifact
- Add introductions and/or reflections to all artifacts
- Create multiple portfolios to meet the needs of different situations
- House a portfolio on the McGraw-Hill server
- Download a portfolio onto their local server (to be burned onto a CD-ROM, etc.)
- Receive support from the McGraw-Hill Help Desk

How To Use *Folio*Live

Introduction 4

Logging-in and Creating Your Account 7

Creating Your Homepage 8

Creating Course Web Pages 12

Creating Custom Designs 17

Creating Frameworks 21

Using *Manage Files* 26

Registering and Managing Students 28

Providing Feedback on Student Portfolios 31

Getting Help 34

INTRODUCTION

The *How to Use* Folio*Live* section describes how to use the instructor's area of Folio*Live*. The section includes:

- *Logging-in and Creating Your Account* (page 7)
- *Creating Your Homepage* (page 8)
- *Creating Course Web Pages* (page 12)
- *Creating Custom Designs* (page 17)
- *Using Manage Files* (page 26)
- *Creating Frameworks* (page 28)
- *Registering Students and Managing Your Course Web Pages* (page 28)
- *Providing Feedback on Student Portfolios* (page 31)
- *Getting Help* (page 34)

To enter the instructor's area, go to **www.foliolive.com** and enter your username and password (for first-time users, see ***Logging-in and Creating Your Account*** on page 7). The instructor's area is organized into four parts: Instructor Menu, Resources, Utility, and Additional.

Instructor Menu

The areas listed under Instructor Menu are those that you will use most frequently.

Start Here provides a quick overview of the instructor's area.

The **My Homepage** area is where you create the homepage from which your courses will be linked. In this area, you choose or edit your homepage design, add an introductory statement, select whether you want your email address displayed, password protect your site, and activate your homepage.

The **My Courses** area is where you can create Web sites for your individual courses. For each course, you choose a Web site design, enter course information, and create a student registration password. By clicking on a course listed in this area, you can view a listing of students who have "joined" the course through Folio*Live*, activate or deactivate individual students, and provide feedback on student portfolios and artifacts.

The **My Frameworks** area allows you to create Frameworks (portfolio tables of contents) for your students to use. By "joining" your course, students will have access to your active Frameworks.

Resources

The **Resources** area contains information for you to reference as you use *Folio*Live.

Utility

The **My Account** area allows you to see how much time is left in your account, check the amount of server space you have used and have remaining, and change your account log-in and contact information.

The **Manage Files** area houses all of the files you upload or create. This area allows you to upload additional files and to manage your existing files.

Student Mode links you to the student version of *Folio*Live so you can view the tool your students are using and optionally create a sample portfolio.

Additional

The **Help** section includes detailed instructions for using *Folio*Live's instructor's tools, as well as *Frequently Asked Questions* and Help Desk contact information.

Log Out allows you to log-out of your *Folio*Live account and returns you to the *Folio*Live homepage.

LOGGING-IN AND CREATING YOUR ACCOUNT

To create your account, go to **www.foliolive.com** and click "Instructors – Click here to REGISTER."

Follow the directions on each screen. At the end of the process, your user-name and password will be emailed to you.

To log-on to *Folio*Live, go to **www.foliolive.com** and enter your username and password.

CREATING YOUR HOMEPAGE

Your homepage will list each of your courses, as well as any introductory material you choose to add.

Establish Your Homepage

To establish your homepage, click "My Homepage" on the left-hand menu. First, you must select a design under "Homepage Designs." You can choose a *Folio*Live provided design, or you can create a custom design (see *Creating Custom Designs* on page 17). After selecting a design, click "Save."

To view your homepage, click the URL following "Your Web Site Address" at the top of the screen.

> **Your Web Site Address**
> **http://demo-i.foliolive.net**

To change your URL, go to the My Account area and click "Change Your Web Site Address."

Choose or Create a Homepage Design

You have the option of choosing a *Folio*Live provided design or creating a custom design for your homepage.

To choose a *Folio*Live template design, click "*Folio*Live provided designs" and select the design you wish to use from the pull-down menu. Click "Save." To preview these designs, click on the link entitled "Preview *Folio*Live Provided Designs."

To create a custom design, see *Creating Custom Designs* on page 17.

> **Homepage Design**
> Select a *Folio***Live** design or create a custom design for your homepage.
> Preview *FolioL**ive** Provided Designs
>
> ○ FolioLive provided designs   [Default Instructor ⬍]
>
> ◉ My designs   [Prof Smith's Design ⬍] [Create/Edit My Designs]

Add an Image

To add an image, go to the "My Image" section of the page. Select either "Upload Image" or "Select Existing Image" based on whether you have previously uploaded the image that you want to use to *Folio*Live.

Upload Image: After clicking "Upload Image," click "Browse" to select the image you want to upload from your local system. After the path to the image is listed in the box, click "Upload."

Note that there is a chart on the bottom of the screen that provides estimated upload times based on the size of the file and the connection speed of your computer to the Internet.

Select Existing Image: After clicking "Select Existing Image," click here if you have previously uploaded the image you wish to add to *Folio*Live. At the next screen, select the image you wish to use and click "Select Image."

The image that you selected will be listed in the box next to "My Image." Click "Save."

My Image
Select an image to be displayed as part of your introduction.

| /nancy.jpg | Upload Image | Select Existing Image |

Add an Introductory Statement

To add an Introductory Statement, scroll to the "Introductory Statement" section of the page. Type your statement directly into the text box. Click "Save."

To use HTML code within this box, select the "Text includes HTML formatting" box. HTML formatting allows you to use "tags" to modify text so that you can bold, italicize, indent, and create hotlinks to the Internet. Click "Formatting Tips" for a list of common tags and their uses.

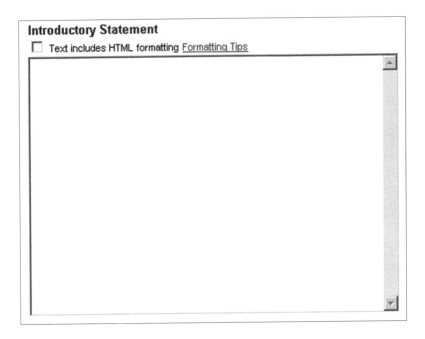

Add Your Email Address

To list your email address on your homepage, check the "Show My Email Address as a Link" box. The email that you provided during your registration process will be added to your homepage. To change your email address, go to the "My Account" area. Click "Save."

☑ **Show my e-mail address as a link**

Password Protect Your Homepage

To password protect your homepage, enter the password in the box following "Homepage Password." If you enter a password here, viewers will need to know it to gain access to your site. Click "Save."

Homepage Password
By providing a password here, viewers would be required to know that password in order to view your site.

Activate Your Homepage

Your homepage will only be viewable through the Internet if it is "Active." You may wish to keep it inactive until you have finalized it and added your courses.

To Activate your homepage, click the "Web Site Active" box. Click "Save."

☑ **Web Site Active**
By placing a check mark in the Web Site Active box, you are enabling the Web site to be viewed.

CREATING COURSE WEB PAGES

*Folio*Live allows you to create a Web page for each of your courses.

To add or edit a course, click "My Courses" on the left hand menu.

Add a Course

To add a course, go to the "My Courses" area and click "Add a New Course." Enter the course title next to "Course Title" and choose a *Folio*Live template design or create a custom design (see **Creating Custom Designs** on page 17). Optional material that you can add includes a page instruction and a course description. You may also activate your course Web page and add a registration password. **To save the course,** click "Add Course."

Add New Course

To view your course, click the URL following "Your Web Site Address" at the top of the screen and click the course you want to view.

There are several optional features you can add to your course Web page.

Choose or Create a Course Design

You have the option of choosing a *Folio*Live template design or creating a custom design for your course Web page.

To choose a *Folio*Live template design, click "*Folio*Live template designs" and select the design you wish to use from the pull-down menu. To preview these designs, click on the link entitled "Preview *Folio*Live Provided Designs."

To create a custom design, see **Creating Custom Designs** on page 17.

Homepage Design
Select a *Folio***Live** design or create a custom design for your homepage.
Preview *FolioLive* Provided Designs
⦿ *Folio***Live provided designs** | Default Instructor ⬍ |

Add Page Instructions

Page Instruction can be a general introduction, or specific directions for the student.

To add Page Instructions, type the text you would like to appear in the "Page Instruction" text field.

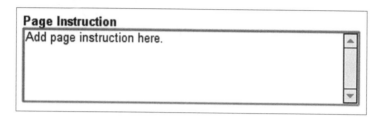

Add a Course Description

To add a Course Description, type the text you would like to appear in the "Course Description" field.

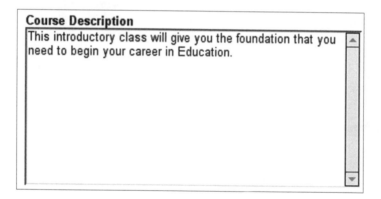

Activate Your Course

Your course Web page is only viewable through the Internet (and posted on your homepage) if it is "Active." You may wish to keep it inactive until you have finalized your course Web page.

To activate your course Web page, click the box next to "Course is Active." You can also activate or deactivate your course from the "My Courses" page by checking the box next to the course title and clicking the "Activate" or "Deactivate" button.

Title	Students Registered	Status	Closed Registration
☐ EDU 101 Intro to Education	1	Active	No
☐ EDU 210 The Pursuit of Classroom Excellence	0	Active	No
☑ EDU 410 Advanced Teaching Skills	0	Active	No
☐ **Select All**			

[Activate]   Activate the selected courses.
[Deactivate] Deactivate the selected courses.

Add a Registration Password

You have the option of requiring a password for students to register for your course (for more on registering students, see ***Registering Students and Managing Your Course Web Pages*** on page 28). If you choose to use a password, your students will have to enter this password before being able to join your course.

To add a registration password, enter the password in the "Registration Password" box.

Registration Password
[_____]

Close Registration

You can prevent registration to your *Folio*Live course by Closing Registration.

To Close Registration, check the box next to "Close Registration."

Close Registration
Close registration controls whether students can register for your course.

- Check **Close Registration** to close the registration.
- Uncheck **Close Registration** to allow students to register.

☐ Close Registration.

Automatic Activation

You have the option of approving each student who registers for your course, or allowing students to automatically be added to your *Folio*Live course after they register for it (see *Registering Students and Managing Your Course Web Pages* on page 28).

To activate Automatic Activation, check the box next to "Automatic Activation."

Automatic Activation
Automatic activation controls whether students will be automatically activated when they register for your course.

- Check **Automatic Activation** to automatically activate students.
- Uncheck **Automatic Activation** to manually activate students after they have registered.

☑ Automatic Activation

Edit an Existing Course

To edit an existing course, go to the "My Courses" area and click on the title of the course you want to edit. Follow the directions on pages 12 through 15 to make specific changes. Click "Save Course" at the bottom of the page when you have finished to save any changes.

Title	Students Registered	Status	Closed Registration
☐ EDU 101 Intro to Education	1	Active	No
☐ EDU 210 The Pursuit of Classroom Excellence	0	Active	No
☐ EDU 410 Advanced Teaching Skills	0	Active	No
☐ **Select All**			

[Activate]   Activate the selected courses.

[Deactivate] Deactivate the selected courses.

CREATING CUSTOM DESIGNS

You have the option of creating a custom design for both your homepage and each of your course Web pages.

If creating a custom design for your homepage, start at "My Homepage."

If creating a custom design for a course Web page go to "My Courses" and click on the title of the course to which you want to add the design.

To create a custom design, click "Create/Edit My Designs." Click "Create New Design." Input a title for your design, and click "Continue."

[Create/Edit My Designs]

My Designs

To create a custom design for your homepage, click "Create New Design".

To edit an existing design, click on the design title below.

[Create New Design]

My Designs

To create a new page design, enter a title for the design and then click "Continue". To cancel and return to the "My Designs" page, click "Back."

Design Title (required)

School Design

[<< Back] [Continue >>]

The "Specify Page Design Attributes" page allows you the option to change various elements of the page design. You can modify images such as the Header, Bullets, and Footer, and you can modify the size, color, and style of the fonts.

Design Title: title | Save |

| Preview Homepage |

Homepage Attributes	Current Setting
Homepage Header Image	Not Defined
Homepage Bullet Image	Default Bullet
Homepage Footer Image	No Footer Image
Homepage Title Font	16 pt, Black, Arial
Homepage Text Font	12 pt, Black, Arial
Homepage Background Color	White

| Preview Course Page |

Course Attributes	Current Setting
Course Header Image	Not Defined
Course Bullet Image	Default Bullet
Course Footer Image	No Footer Image

To add an image (in the header or as a bullet), click on the attribute title (for example, Header Image). Choose to upload an image or to select an image that you uploaded previously. Click "Save."

To change the size of the image, enter a new width and length. Click "Save."

To add a link to the image (when the link is clicked, the viewer will be forwarded to another page), enter the URL of the page you want to send viewers to in the "Image Link" box. Click "Save."

To add text that will appear when the mouse is moved over the image, type in the desired text in the "Alternate Text" box. Click "Save."

Add Image for Header

The "Add Image" area allows you to insert your own images on your portfolio web pages. To specify the appearance of your page, please provide the appropriate information below.
Note: Where no changes are made, the default value for the attribute will be used as specified below.

Image Location (required)
To add a new image to your "My Files" area, click on the link below. If you already saved your image to the "My Files" area or elsewhere, you may enter the location for your image below. Please click on "Save" before exiting this page.

[_____] [Upload Image] [Select Existing Image]

Image Width and Height (optional)
The image width and height is optional. To specify a width and height, please do so below. Please click on "Save" before exiting this page.
Note: We recommend a width of no more than 570 pixels.

Width [   ]   **Height** [   ]

To modify text style, click on the desired font attribute (for example, Normal Page Text Font) and select the font size, style, family and color that you would like. Click "Save."

Add Font for Text

The "Add Font" area allows you to define the physical style of the text. To specify the appearance of your text, please make the appropriate selections below. To restore the text to the default font values, click the "Restore Default" button.
Note: Where no changes are made, the default value for the attribute will be used as specified below.

Font Style
By default, the font style is set to **12pt, Bold, Arial, Helvetica.** To change any of these settings, please make your selections below and click on "Save" before exiting this page.

Font Size [12 ⬍]   **Text Style** ☑ **Bold** ☐ *Italic* ☐ Underline

Font Family
◉ Arial, Helvetica ○ Arial, Verdana ○ Sans Serif
○ Serif   ○ Times

To modify the background color of the page, click "Background Color." Select the color you wish to use from the pull-down menu and click "Save."

To preview your custom design, click "Preview Homepage" or "Preview Course Page."

To restore the original settings, click "Restore Default."

To edit a custom design, select "Create/Edit My Designs" on "My Homepage" or "My Courses." Click on the title of the design you wish to edit. Follow the directions above under **To Create a Custom Design** starting on page 17 to make specific edits.

To delete a custom design, select "Create/Edit My Designs" on "My Homepage" or "My Courses." Click on the title of the design you wish to delete. Click "Delete Design" at the bottom of the page.

CREATING FRAMEWORKS

Frameworks are portfolio organizations or tables of contents. *Folio*Live provides several Frameworks that students can use. As the instructor, you can create Frameworks specific to your courses or program. A student who is "joined" to your *Folio*Live course will have access to your Frameworks.

Preview *Folio*Live Frameworks

*Folio*Live provides several Frameworks – primarily based on standards, such as INTASC, NBPTS, ISTE, etc.

To preview *Folio*Live Frameworks, go to the "My Frameworks" area and click "Preview *Folio*Live Frameworks."

Add a Framework

To add a new Framework, go to the "My Frameworks" area and click "Add Framework." Enter a title, and optionally a description (or general explanation of the assignment). Click "Add Framework." Follow the directions below under **Create or Edit a Framework** to construct your Framework.

[Add New Framework]

Add Framework

To add a new Framework, enter its title and a description. Click "Add Framework."

After the Framework has been added, you will be returned to the "My Frameworks" page. In the "My Frameworks" area, click the Framework title to add placeholders.

Title (required)

Description

[Add Framework]

To edit the Framework title and description, click on the Framework name and then click "Edit Framework."

[Edit Framework]

Create or Edit a Framework

A Framework consists of Sections and Placeholders. *Sections* are headings or titles for groups of artifacts. *Placeholders* are areas where artifacts will be added.

To add a Section, click on the title of the Framework you want to add a section to and click "Add New Portfolio Section." Enter the title. If you want the Section to fall under another Section, select it from the "Parent Portfolio Section" pull-down menu. Click "Add Portfolio Section."

[Add New Portfolio Section]

Add Portfolio Section

To add a portfolio section, enter the title and specify whether it is part of a larger parent portfolio section. Click "Add Portfolio Section" when finished.

To add placeholder within the portfolio section, click "Add Placeholder" on the "Frameworks - Placeholders" page.

Title (required)

> General Resources

Parent Portfolio Section

> (none) ♦

> Add Portfolio Section

To add a Placeholder, click on the title of the Framework you want to add a placeholder to and click "Add New Placeholder." Enter the title, and optionally a description (or assignment).

> **To use HTML code within this box,** select the "Text includes HTML formatting" box. HTML formatting allows you to use "tags" to modify text so that you can bold, italicize, indent, and create hotlinks to the Internet. Click "Formatting Tips," for a list of common tags and their uses.

> If you want the Placeholder to fall under a Section, select it from the "Parent Portfolio Section" pull-down menu.

> Click "Add Placeholder."

> Add New Placeholder

To activate or deactivate a Framework, go to the "My Frameworks" area and click the box next to the title of the Framework you would like to change the status of. Click the "activate" or "deactivate" button as appropriate.

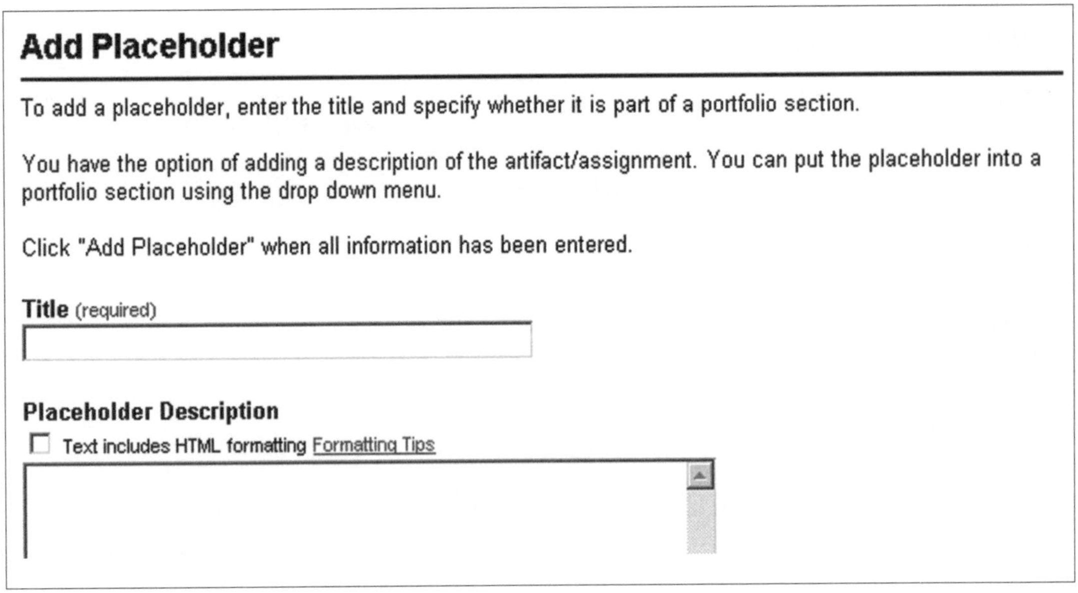
Add Placeholder
To add a placeholder, enter the title and specify whether it is part of a portfolio section.
You have the option of adding a description of the artifact/assignment. You can put the placeholder into a portfolio section using the drop down menu.
Click "Add Placeholder" when all information has been entered.
Title (required)
Placeholder Description
Text includes HTML formatting Formatting Tips

To view placeholders within sections, click the "+."

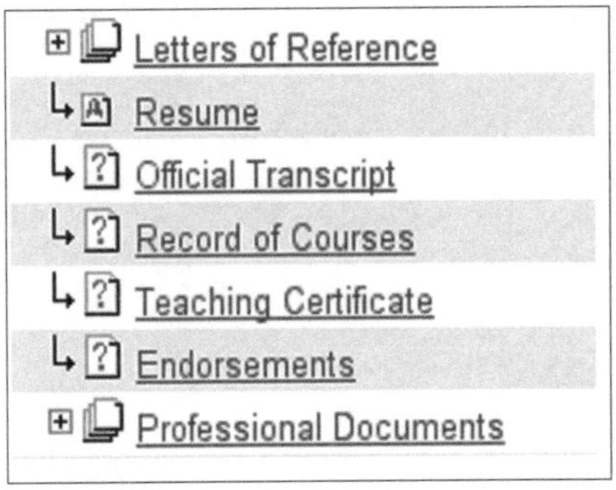
Letters of Reference
Resume
Official Transcript
Record of Courses
Teaching Certificate
Endorsements
Professional Documents

To reorder your Framework, click on the title of the Framework you want to reorder and click "Reorder Framework." Enter the order in which you would like the sections and placeholders to appear.

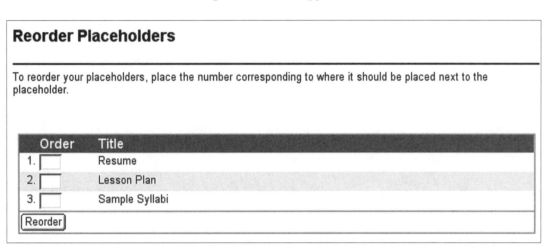

To reorder placeholders within a section, click on the section title from the Reorder Placeholders screen. Enter the order in which you would like the placeholders to appear.

To move a placeholder from one section to another (or out of any section), click on the placeholder name, and then choose where it should be listed from the "Portfolio Section" pull-down menu.

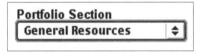

To delete a placeholder, click on the placeholder name, and click "Delete" at the bottom of the page.

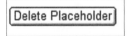

To delete a section, click on the section name, and click "Delete" at the bottom of the page.

Delete Portfolio Section

USING *MANAGE FILES*

"Manage Files" is an area that houses all of the files that you upload into your *Folio*Live account. These will primarily consist of files you upload to create your homepage or custom designs.

To upload a file directly into "Manage Files," go to the "Manage Files" area and click "Add a New File." Click "Browse" to select the image you want to upload from your local system. After the path to the image is visible in the box, click "Upload."

Note that there is a chart on the bottom of the screen that provides estimated upload times based on the size of the file and the connection speed of your computer to the Internet.

Manage Files - Add a New File

Use the Browse button to locate a file on your local system to upload.

[   ] [Browse...]

To create a sub-directory to organize your files, click "Add Sub-Directory." Enter the name for the directory and click "Create Directory."

To move a file into a directory, check the box next to the file and click "Move." Click "Tree View" and select the directory (or folder) you want to move the file into. After this is selected, click "Move."

Manage Files - Move Files to a New Location

Enter the directory path (starting at your root directory: **demo-s**) to the location you would like to move the specified files to or click the "Tree View" button for a fully expanded directory tree to choose from. After selecting a target directory path, click the "Move" at the bottom of the page to perform the operation.

Target Directory Path:
⬜○ demo-s

	Name	Type
☑	⬜ resume.rtf	file

[Move]   Click the "Move" button to move the selected files.
[<< Back]

To rename a file, check the box next to the file name and click "Rename." Enter the new name and click "Rename."

To copy a file, check the box next to the file name and click "Copy." Click "Tree View" and indicate where you want the file copied to. Click "Copy."

To delete a file, check the box next to the file and click "Delete."

Directories		Name	Type	Last Modified MM/DD/YYYY	Size (bytes)
📁 demo-s	⬜ 📄	lessonplan.doc	text	07/24/2002	27,648
	⬜ 🖼	image2.jpg	image	07/24/2002	50,751
	☑ ⬜	resume.rtf	file	07/24/2002	3,210
	⬜ **Select All**				**81,609 bytes**

[Copy] [Move]   Total Space Available   : 5,000,000 bytes
[Delete] [Rename]   Total Space Used   :   81,609 bytes
Total Space Remaining : 4,918,391 bytes

REGISTERING AND MANAGING STUDENTS

When a student "joins" your *Folio*Live course, their portfolio is automatically listed on your course Web page, and they have access to your active Frameworks. You can then provide feedback on the portfolios and artifacts belonging to students joined to your *Folio*Live course (see **Providing Feedback on Student Portfolios** on page 31).

Student Registration

Students register for your *Folio*Live courses through their *Folio*Live accounts. To do this, they click "Join a Course" and *paste in your Homepage URL* and click "Continue." Next, students select which of your courses they want to join, and click "Join." *If you have required a password for course registration, students will have to enter it at this time.*

Join A Course

If you are using *Folio*Live in conjunction with a course, the "Join a Course" feature allows you to link your homepage to your instructor?s *Folio***Live** course Web site.

To "Join a Course," your instructor must provide you with his/her *Folio***Live** course Web site URL(and possibly a password).

You are currently registered for the for the following courses:

	Course Title	Instructor	Status in Course
☐	EDU 101 Intro to Education	Professor Smith	Active
☐	**Select All**		

[Detach] Detach from the selected course(s).

To join a course, enter your instructor's *Folio***Live** Web site address and click "Continue."
Instructor's *Folio*Live URL (required)

http://demo-i.foliolive.net

[Continue >>]

To view the students who have joined your course, go to the "My Courses" area and click the course title.

If you did not select Automatic Registration for your course when you created the course in "My Courses," you will need to activate individual students as they join the course.

Students for Course: EDU 101 Intro to Education

Below is a list of the students who have registered for your course. Only the students who have registered for your course and have an active status will have their homepages linked to your course Web site. As the instructor, you can change a student's status by selecting the student and clicking "Activate" or "Deactivate."

To provide feedback on a student's portfolio and artifacts, go to their Web site and click "Provide Feedback" on the page you want to comment on. This will generate an email to the student that includes a reference and link to the page you are commenting on.

[Edit Course] [Edit Web Links]

	Name	Login	Status
☐	Jones, Nancy	demo-s	Active
☐	**Select All**		

[Activate]　Activate the selected students for this course.

[Deactivate]　Deactivate the selected students for this course.

[Remove]　Remove the selected students from this course.

To edit the Automatic Registration feature from this point, click on "Edit Course."

To activate a student, click on the course name. Check the box next to the student's name and click "Activate."

To deactivate a student, check the box next to the student's name and click "Deactivate."

To remove a student, check the box next to the student's name and click "Remove."

	Name	Login	Status
☐	Jones, Nancy	demo-s	Active
☐	**Select All**		

[Activate]   Activate the selected students for this course.

[Deactivate] Deactivate the selected students for this course.

[Remove]   Remove the selected students from this course.

PROVIDING FEEDBACK ON STUDENT PORTFOLIOS

*Folio*Live allows you to provide feedback to students on their portfolios and artifacts.

Provide Feedback

To comment on a student's portfolio or artifact, go to "My Courses" and click on the course in which the student is registered. Next, click on the student's name. This will point you to the student's homepage. Click on the portfolio on which you want to comment.

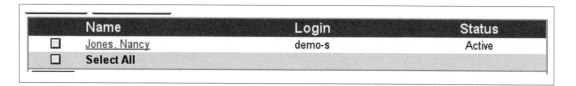

	Name	Login	Status
☐	Jones, Nancy	demo-s	Active
☐	**Select All**		

To comment on the entire portfolio, click "Provide Feedback" located in the top right corner of the portfolio.

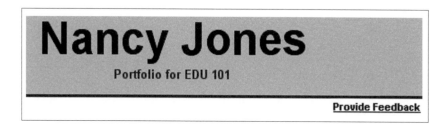

To comment on a specific artifact or section of artifacts, navigate to the section or artifact using the menu on the left-hand side. Click "Provide Feedback" when you are on the page on which you want to comment.

A feedback form will appear. You will need to fill in who the feedback is from (it defaults to the information you provided during registration), the subject, and the feedback. You also have the option of sending yourself a copy of the message.

Portfolio Feedback

This page allows you to give feedback on an artifact in your student's portfolio. The feedback is sent as an e-mail to the student. You have the ability to copy the e-mail to your own e-mail address for your records.

From (required)

Professor Smith   (prof_smith@anyschool.edu)

Subject (required)

Context for Student
This is feedback for your artifact entitled: Home
that resides within your portfolio: Portfolio for EDU 101.

Reference: http://demo-s.foliolive.net/portfolio/start?portfoliold=256

Feedback (required)

☐ **For my records, send a copy my to e-mail address.**

[Send]

To send yourself a copy of the message, click the box next to "For my records, send a copy to my email address."

The feedback will be sent to the email address that the student used during registration. For easy reference, the link to the page you commented on will be included in the email.

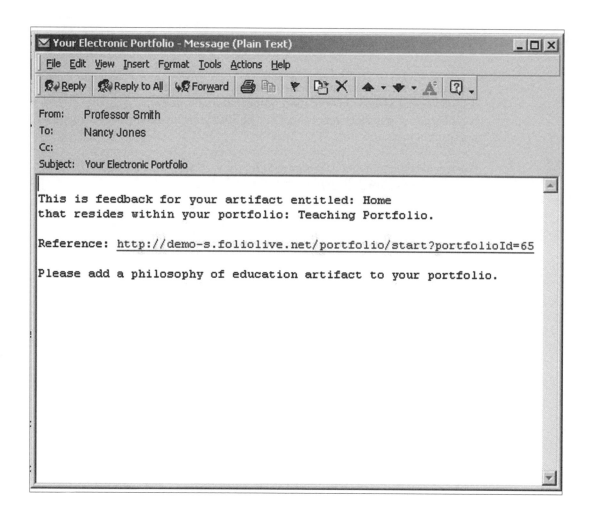

GETTING HELP

To order *Folio*Live, obtain an instructor's desk passcode, or to request a demonstration of *Folio*Live or more information about *Folio*Live, contact your local McGraw-Hill sales representative. To find your local representative, go to www.mhhe.com and click "Rep Locator."

For technical help, contact McGraw-Hill Software Support at 1-800-331-5094 or techsup@mcgraw-hill.com, or visit the Help Desk at www.mhhe.com/helpdesk.

The Help Desk is open from 8:00am to 5:30pmCST.

APPENDIX: USER'S GUIDE TO FolioLive

GLOSSARY

Artifact: Any item included in a portfolio used as tangible evidence of ability or accomplishment.

Custom Portfolio: In *Folio*Live, a portfolio that the user creates from scratch.

Electronic Portfolio: A portfolio that consists of electronic files – whether online, on a CD-ROM, or a local network.

Framework: In *Folio*Live, a portfolio table of contents (or outline) that includes suggestions for artifacts. It is a template for creating a portfolio by linking actual artifacts to the placeholders for suggested artifacts. A Framework consists of a group of placeholders.

Framework Portfolio: In *Folio*Live, a portfolio that the user creates based on a Framework.

Placeholder: In *Folio*Live, indicates where an artifact should be placed. A group of placeholders is a Framework.

Portfolio: A purposeful collection of your best teaching efforts.

Section: In *Folio*Live, a group of artifacts.

Sub-Directory: In *Folio*Live, a group of files in *Manage Files*.

INDEX

Account creation, 7
Activate
   course Web page, 11
   Framework, 23
   Homepage, 11
Additional, 5
Artifact, 37
   feedback on student's, 31–33
Automatic activation, 15, 29

Background color, 20
Benefits of *Folio*Live
   for instructor, ix
   for student, ix–x
Close Registration, 15
Course Management, *see also*
   Registration *and* Join a Course,
   28–30
   activate student, 29
   automatic activation, 15, 29
   deactivate student, 29
   remove student, 30
   view registered students, 29
Course Web Page, 12–16
   activate, 13–14
   add or edit a course Web page, 12
   automatic activation, 15
   close registration, 15
   course description, 13
   deactivate, 13–14
   design, 12, 17–20
   edit course Web page, 16
   page instructions, 13
   registration password, 14
   view, 12

Design,
   course Web page, 12
   custom, 17–20
     background color, 20
     create, 17
     delete, 20
     edit, 20
     image, 18
     page design attributes, 18
     preview, 20
     restore settings, 20
     text style, 19
   *Folio*Live provided, 8, 12
   homepage, 8
Desk passcode, v

Email address, 10
Feedback, 31–33
   form, instructor, 32
   form, received by student, 33
   student artifacts, on, 31
   student portfolio, on, 31
Frameworks, 21–25, 37
   activate, 23
   add new, 21–25
   deactivate, 23
   delete placeholder, 25
   delete section, 25
   edit, 22
   *Folio*Live provided, preview, 21
   placeholder, add, 23–24
   portfolio section, add, 22–23
     parent portfolio section, 23
   reorder, 25
   title, 21

Help, 5, 34
   demonstration or training, 34
   ordering assistance, 34
   technical help, 34
Help Desk, contact information, 34
Homepage, 8–11
   activate, 11
   create a homepage, 8–11
   deactivate, 11
   design, 8, 17–20
   email address, 10
   image, 9
   Introductory Statement, 9–10
   password protection, 11
   view, 8
HTML
   introductory statement, 10
   placeholder description, 23
Image
   bullet, add to, 18
     add alternate text, 19
     add link, 18
     change size, 18
   course Web page, add to, 18
   footer, add to, 18
     add alternate text, 19
     add link, 18
     change size, 18
   header, add to, 18
     add alternate text, 19
     add link, 18
     change size, 18
   homepage, add to, 9

Instructor Menu, 4
Introductory Statement, 9–10

Join a Course, *see also* Registration *and*
   Course Management, 28–30

Logging-in, 7
Log Out, 6

Manage Files, 5
   copy file, 27
   delete file, 27
   move file into sub-directory, 27
   rename file, 27
   sub-directory, 26
   upload file, 26
My Account, 5
   email, 10
   URL, 10
My Courses, 4
My Frameworks, 5
My Homepage, 4

Ordering information, v

Page design attributes, 18
Password protection
   course Web page, 14
   homepage, 11
   registration, 14
Placeholder, 37
   add, 23–24
   delete, 25
   reorder, 25
   view within section, 24
Portfolio
   feedback on student's, 31–33
   view student, 31

Registration, instructor, 7
Registration, student, *see also* Join a Course
   and Course Management, 28–30
   automatic activation, 15
   close, 15
   deactivate student, 29
   password, 14
   remove student, 30
   student registration, 28
Resources, 5

Sales representative, v
Section, 37

add to Framework, 22–23
delete, 25
parent Portfolio Section, 23
reorder, 25
view placeholders within, 24
Start Here, 4
Student Mode, 5
Student portfolios
feedback, 31–33

viewing, 31
Sub-directory, 37
create, 26
move file into, 27

Text style, 19

URL, 8
Utility, *5*

USER'S GUIDE TO *FOLIO*LIVE

TABLE OF CONTENTS

Preface v

Why Create a Portfolio? Why Create an Electronic Portfolio? 1

An Overview of *Folio*Live 3

How To Use *Folio*Live. 5
Introduction 6
Logging-in and Creating Your Account 9
Creating Your Homepage 10
Creating a Portfolio 13
Creating Custom Designs 28
Using Frameworks and Standards 32
Using *Manage Files* 35
Using *Manage Artifacts* 37
Joining a Course 39
Downloading Your Portfolio 40
Managing Your *Folio*Live Account 41
Getting Help 42

Developing and Maintaining Your Electronic Portfolio 43

Glossary. 45

Index 47

PREFACE

INTRODUCING *FOLIO*LIVE

Increasingly, pre-service teachers are building portfolios in teacher training programs and continuing to develop them throughout their teaching careers. As technology becomes an integral part of education, a logical progression has been to make portfolios available electronically. "More and more institutions are encouraging — or even requiring — students to create 'electronic portfolios' that highlight their academic work and help them reflect on their campus experiences." This quotation begins Jeffrey R. Young's article "Creating Online Portfolios Can Help Students See 'Big Picture,' Colleges Say," published in the February 21, 2002 edition of *The Chronicle of Higher Education.* This article provided an impetus for the creation of *Folio*Live. Instructors in numerous schools of education have wanted to use electronic portfolios in their courses, but have found obstacles such as insufficient technical knowledge, limited school resources, and a lack of time to invest in creating and supporting an e-portfolio system kept them from doing so. *Folio*Live answers the needs of these instructors and universities, and their students, by providing an easy way to create, evaluate, and maintain electronic portfolios.

THE STORY OF *FOLIO*LIVE: THE PEOPLE

McGraw-Hill began the development of *Folio*Live by posing a series of questions to several instructors already using electronic portfolios in their courses. These instructors were asked what capabilities they wanted in an electronic portfolio tool and what features would be most beneficial to have in such a tool. They answered that they wanted an electronic portfolio tool that allowed students to:

- Upload any type of file
- Organize artifacts around standards
- Have multiple portfolios to meet the needs of different situations
- Add introductions and/or reflections to each artifact

The tool should:

- Be easy to use
- Have a Help Desk to answer students' technical questions
- Be affordably priced (the approximate cost of a brief textbook)
- Be available online, but allow students to download their portfolios and burn them onto a CD-Rom
- Allow the instructor to provide feedback directly to each student
- Have a user guide

Using the feedback provided by this group of expert instructors, McGraw-Hill created a preliminary version of *Folio*Live which was then reviewed by a larger group of instructors. This second review produced a wealth of feedback that helped finalize *Folio*Live. Professors who participated in demonstrations of *Folio*Live at the annual meeting of the American Educational Research Association (AERA) in April 2002 in turn provided additional feedback on how *Folio*Live could be revised to meet their needs.

McGraw-Hill would like to take this opportunity to acknowledge the instructors who provided valuable guidance and feedback during the development of *Folio*Live:

Kerri Johnson, *University of Washington*
Natalie B. Milman, *George Washington University*
Cris E. Guenter, *California State University, Chico*
Diane E. Newby, *Central Michigan University*
Mary Elizabeth Hrabe, *University of Virginia*
Tricia Ryan, *Towson University*
Jerry P. Galloway, *Indiana University Northwest*
Joyce Morris, *University of Vermont*
Kristie Walsdorf, *Florida State University*
Iris D. Johnson, *Miami University*
Brenda Frieden, *Pittsburg State University*
Lori A. Norton-Meier, *Kansas State University*
Vickie Williams, *University of Maryland Baltimore County*
V. Vanese Delahoussaye, *Houston Community College*
Paul Walsh, *Johns Hopkins University*
Leslie J. Davison, *St. Cloud State University*
Saundra L. Wetig, *University of Nebraska at Omaha*
Frank Guldbrandsen, *University of Minnesota*

THE STORY OF *FOLIO*LIVE: THE TECHNOLOGY

A key goal of McGraw-Hill Higher Education's mission is to provide quality content and technology-enhanced delivery of instructional content and services. As a leading college publisher, McGraw-Hill has dedicated vast resources to producing technology products and instructor support materials which align both students and instructors with the technological demands of today's classrooms and their future work environment. McGraw-Hill is dedicated to providing technology products such as *Folio*Live that support instructors and allow students to expand their learning.

*Folio*Live is based on the proven technology of McGraw-Hill's highly successful PageOut course management product. Launched in 1999, PageOut is currently in use by over 60,000 instructors.

BENEFITS TO THE USERS

*Folio*Live allows users to easily create professional-looking electronic portfolios. The user can:

- **Create an electronic portfolio in a few simple steps.** The user creates a portfolio by choosing to create a custom or Framework portfolio, selecting a design, and then adding artifacts (uploading existing files or creating new artifacts through a *Folio*Live template).
- **Easily organize portfolios around standards.** *Folio*Live Frameworks based on key standards (such as INTASC, NBPTS, and ISTE) allow the easy construction of portfolios based on standards.
- **Create multiple electronic portfolios.** The user can construct several portfolios to meet the needs of different situations. For example, a user might have a course portfolio, an INTASC portfolio, and an interview portfolio.
- **Add introductions and/or reflections to each artifact.** Users can add introductions and/or artifacts to each artifact to demonstrate growth and reflection.
- **Download their portfolios.** Users can download their portfolios onto their local systems to burn onto a CD-ROM.
- **Get support from a McGraw-Hill Help Desk.** The McGraw-Hill Help desk is available to help users with lost passwords and technical questions.

YOUR INVOLVEMENT WITH *FolioLive*

Classroom instructors have already played an important role in the development of *Folio*Live. We now invite *you* to become involved with *Folio*Live. Let us know how well *Folio*Live meets your needs. What capabilities would you add? How has it helped in your development? Email us your feedback at **education@mcgraw-hill.com.**

WHY CREATE A PORTFOLIO? WHY CREATE AN ELECTRONIC PORTFOLIO?*

How Portfolios Benefit You

As you complete your course credits, hours of study, and years of experience in college and in your pre-service student teaching endeavors, you are continually accumulating a vast array of outstanding examples of your growth as an educator. You have papers of which you are particularly proud, glowing narrative descriptions of your first time in front of a group of students, and critical but encouraging evaluations from your supervisors. Most important, you will have documentation that you possess both the desire and the knowledge necessary to become a dedicated professional and a life-long learner.

Another personal reason to maintain portfolios is to keep records of the wonderful projects, bulletin boards, learning centers, and thematic units you have created. As the years fly by, the memories of these unique creations will fade and you will find yourself wishing you had kept copies of them to adapt for future students. You may become an experienced educator who wishes to teach in a different area and could finally use all those projects you learned about and created but never got the chance to pursue when you were an undergraduate. Or you may take post-graduate classes and want to refer to all those wonderful activities you implemented when you student taught.

Finally, teaching portfolios provide opportunities for reflection. Reflection is the ability and disposition to think deeply and make decisions about which strategy is appropriate at any given time. It is easy to get so swept up in the day-to-day (or minute-to-minute) hectic world of teaching that you forget to stop and think about how your lessons have turned out, or how you feel about the day's events. Maintaining a portfolio gives you the opportunity to develop the healthy habit of reflecting on the success (or lack thereof) of a lesson. Saving student work that demonstrates learning validates your work, your planning, your lesson and reminds you why it worked. On the other hand, saving student work that shows how the lesson failed provides valuable input as well. You can learn from your mistakes and chuckle as you come across the unfortunate samples years later. Either way, you are taking the time to consider the effects of your efforts—isn't that what we always wish for our students to do?

---

* Based on Rieman, Patricia. *Teaching Portfolios: Presenting Your Professional Best.* New York: McGraw-Hill, 2000.

How Portfolios Benefit Your Prospective Employers

Employers who are seeking new employees to join their staffs are in precarious positions. They must rely on subjective evaluations such as interviews, letters of recommendation from people who are strangers to them, and the word — possibly lip service — of those being interviewed. The opportunity to see and to have the time to read and reflect upon a professional portfolio gives employers the chance to affirm or discredit their intuition with hard facts. The professional portfolio eliminates doubt and reinforces the recommendations given by you and your personal references. While employers may not have the time or the opportunity to examine each and every portfolio that comes their way, they may have certain criteria in mind as they skim through the artifacts. Another way you can use the portfolio as you interview is to organize it neatly so that you can immediately pull out a certain section as the topic arises in the interview.

Employers must weed out the sincere from the false, the knowledgeable from the vague, and the genuinely best qualified from the best-worded applicants. Portfolios provide authentic assessment of an educator's skills, accomplishments, and teaching philosophy. Portfolios may include glowing letters of thanks from parents or students, awards from the school or community, and certificates of additional coursework completed. These artifacts compiled with complimentary letters of reference and moving personal statements all give employers a fair representation of exactly whom they are considering.

Why Create an Electronic Portfolio?

There are several benefits to creating an electronic portfolio, in addition to, or instead of, a traditional paper portfolio:

1. You can easily and safely share your portfolio with several people without having to make duplicate portfolios or worrying about your portfolio being lost or damaged.
2. Viewers can access your electronic portfolio easily and quickly whether you give them a URL or CD-ROM.
3. You can reorganize your artifacts to create multiple portfolios that fit different situations (for a class requirement, a job interview, etc.) without much effort.
4. Video and audio artifacts can be easily included in an electronic portfolio.
5. Creating an electronic portfolio allows you to demonstrate your proficiency in using technology.
6. You can easily update your portfolio, and keep it looking current by changing its design.
7. Artifacts never look worn or old.

An Overview of *Folio*Live

*Folio*Live allows users to easily create professional-looking electronic portfolios. The user can:

- Create a Homepage
- Create a professional-looking electronic portfolio
- Create a custom portfolio or use a *Folio*Live Framework
- Easily organize a portfolio around standards using a *Folio*Live Framework or by creating a custom portfolio
- Upload any type of file (from Word to PowerPoint to audio to video) to be used as an artifact
- Add introductions and/or reflections to all artifacts
- Create multiple portfolios to meet the needs of different situations
- Download portfolios to be burned onto a CD-ROM

The user receives space on the McGraw-Hill server, and is supported by a Help Desk. Access is purchased and renewed in one-year increments.

How To Use *Folio*Live

Introduction 6

Logging-in and Creating Your Account 9

Creating Your Homepage 10

Creating a Portfolio 13

Creating Custom Designs 28

Using Frameworks and Standards 32

Using *Manage Files* 35

Using *Manage Artifacts* 37

Joining a Course 39

Downloading Your Portfolio 40

Managing Your *Folio*Live Account 41

Getting Help 42

INTRODUCTION

The *How to Use* Folio*Live* section describes how to create and manage electronic portfolios using *Folio*Live. The sections include:

- Logging-in and Creating Your Account (page 9)
- Creating Your Homepage (page 10)
- Creating a Portfolio (page 13)
- Creating Custom Designs (page 28)
- Using Frameworks and Standards (page 32)
- Using *Manage Files* (page 35)
- Using *Manage Artifacts* (page 37)
- Joining a Course (page 39)
- Managing Your *Folio*Live Account (page 41)
- Getting Help (page 42)

To enter *Folio*Live, go to **www.foliolive.com** and enter your username and password (for first-time users see *Logging-in and Creating Your Account* on page 9). *Folio*Live is organized into four parts:

Authoring

The areas listed under Authoring are those that you will use the most frequently.

Start Here provides a quick overview of the *Folio*Live site.

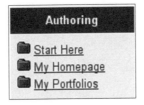

The **My Homepage** area is where you create the homepage from which your portfolios will be linked. In this area you choose or edit your homepage design and can add an introductory statement, select whether you want your email address displayed, password protect your site, and activate your homepage.

The **My Portfolios** area is where you create and manage your electronic portfolios. To create a new portfolio, you choose to create a custom portfolio or to use a *Folio*Live Framework (a portfolio organization with suggested artifacts). For each portfolio you can choose to use a *Folio*Live template design or to create a custom design. After you set up a portfolio, you can add artifacts to it in this area as well.

Resources

The **Resources** area contains documents meant to aid you in the development of your portfolios. These include documents such as: "What Goes into a Teaching Portfolio," "Using Standards to Construct Your Portfolio," "The Need for Reflection," "Recognizing and Expressing Your Philosophy," as well as others.

Utility

The **My Account** area allows you to see how much time is left in your account, check the amount of server space you have used and have remaining, and change your account log-in and contact information.

The **Join a Course** area is where you can link your homepage and portfolios to your instructor's *Folio*Live course, if assigned to do so. By "joining" your instructor's course, your homepage will be linked to their *Folio*Live course Web site and you will have access to your instructor's Frameworks.

The **Download Portfolio** area is where you can download your electronic portfolio onto your local system. From your local system, you can burn it onto a CD-ROM.

The **Manage Artifacts** area houses all of the artifacts that you have uploaded either through My Portfolios or through Manage Artifacts. This area allows you to add additional artifacts (rather than doing so through the My Portfolios area), and to manage your existing artifacts.

The **Manage Files** area houses all of the files you have uploaded or created. This area allows you to upload additional files and to manage your existing files.

Additional

The **Help** area includes detailed instructions for using *Folio*Live and Help Desk contact information.

Log Out allows you to log-out of your *Folio*Live account, and returns you to the *Folio*Live main homepage.

LOGGING-IN AND CREATING YOUR ACCOUNT

To create your account, go to www.foliolive.com and click "Users – Click here to REGISTER."

Follow the directions on each screen. At the end of the process, your user-name and password will be emailed to you.

If you are registering for the first time using the passcode card found in this manual, you can also click "If you purchased a textbook with a special code, please click here."

To log-on to *Folio*Live, go to www.foliolive.com and enter your username and password in the spaces on the left-hand side.

To renew access to *Folio*Live, go to the My Account area and click "Renew."

You will receive notification as to when your account will expire as that time draws near.

CREATING YOUR HOMEPAGE

Your homepage will list your portfolios, as well as any introductory material you choose to add.

To create your homepage, click "My Homepage" on the left-hand menu. To establish your homepage, you need to select a design under "Homepage Designs." You can choose a *Folio*Live template, or you can create a custom design (see **Creating Custom Designs** on page 28). After selecting a design, and clicking "Save," you will be able to view your homepage by clicking the URL following "Your Web Site Address" at the top of the screen.

> **Your Web Site Address**
> **http://demo-s.foliolive.com**

To change your URL, go to the My Account are and click "Change Your Web Site Address."

Choose or Create a Homepage Design

You have the option of choosing a *Folio*Live template design or creating a custom design for your homepage.

To choose a *Folio*Live template design, click "*Folio*Live provided designs" and select the design you wish to use from the pull-down menu. Click "Save." To preview these designs, click on the link entitled "Preview *Folio*Live Provided Designs."

To create a custom design, see **Creating Custom Designs** on page 28.

> **Homepage Design**
> Select a *Folio*Live design or create a custom design for your homepage.
> Preview *Folio*Live Provided Designs
> ● **FolioLive provided designs**   [School Bus ♦]
> ○ **My designs**   [my design ♦] [Create/Edit My Designs]

Add an Image

To add an image to your homepage, go to the "My Image" section of the page. Select either "Upload Image" or "Select Existing Image." Choose "Select Existing Image" if you have uploaded the image previously.

Upload Image: After selecting "Upload Image," click "Browse" to select the image you want to upload from your local system. Next, after the path to the image is visible in the box, click "Upload."

Note that there is a chart on the bottom of the screen that provides estimated upload times based on the size of the file and the connection speed of your computer to the Internet.

Select Existing Image: After selecting "Select Existing Image," select the image you wish to use and click "Select Image."

The image that you selected will be listed in the box next to "Upload Image." Click "Save."

My Image
Select an image to be displayed as part of your introduction.

| /nancy.jpg | Upload Image | Select Existing Image |

Add an Introductory Statement

To add an Introductory Statement, go to the "Introductory Statement" section of the page. Type your statement directly into the text box. Click "Save."

To use HTML code within this box, check the "Text includes HTML formatting" box. HTML formatting allows you to use "tags" to modify text so that you can bold, italicize, indent, and create hotlinks to the Internet. Click "Formatting Tips," for a list of common tags and their uses.

Introductory Statement
☐ Text includes HTML formatting Formatting Tips

Type your introductory statement here.

Add Your Email Address

To list your email address on your homepage, check the "Show My Email Address as a Link" box. The email that you provided during your registration process will be added to your homepage. Click "Save." To change your email address, go to the "My Account" area.

```
☑ Show my e-mail address as a link
```

Password Protect Your Homepage

To password protect your homepage, enter the password in the box following "Homepage Password." Click "Save." If you enter a password here, viewers will need to know it to gain access to your site.

```
Homepage Password
By providing a password here, viewers would be required to know that password in order to view your site.
[                    ]
```

Activate Your Homepage

Your homepage will only be viewable through the Internet if it is "Active." You may wish to keep it inactive until you have finalized your homepage and added portfolios.

To Activate your homepage, click the "Web Site Active" box. Click "Save."

```
☑ Web Site Active
By placing a check mark in the Web Site Active box, you are enabling the Web site to be viewed.

[Save]
```

CREATING A PORTFOLIO

Create a New Portfolio

To create a new portfolio, go to the "My Portfolios" area. You have the option of creating a custom portfolio (with your own organization) or a portfolio based on a Framework. A *Framework* is a portfolio organization (table of contents) with suggested artifacts. *Folio*Live provides several Frameworks for you to choose from (primarily standards-based). If you are using *Folio*Live in a course, your instructor may assign a specific Framework for you to use.

New Portfolio: [Create Custom Portfolio] [Create Portfolio from Framework]

To create a custom portfolio, click "Create Custom Portfolio" at the bottom of the page. On the next page, enter the title and click "Add Portfolio."

Title (required)

[Add Portfolio]

To create a portfolio using a Framework, click "Create Portfolio Using Framework" at the bottom of the page. On the next page, enter your portfolio title, and select the Framework you wish to use. Click "Add Portfolio." To preview the Framework, click the Framework title.

Create Portfolio Using a Framework

To add a portfolio using a Framework, enter a title for the portfolio, and select a Framework from the list below. To preview the Framework, click on its title below. After selecting a Framework, click "Add Portfolio."

Portfolio Title (required)

[   ]

Framework	Provided By
○ INTASC: Interstate New Teacher Assessment and Support Consortium The Interstate New Teacher Assessment and Support Consortium (INTASC) has identified ten standards for what beginning teachers should know. It is noteworthy to add that the National Council for Accreditation of Teacher Education (NCATE) uses the INTASC standards to evaluate teacher education programs.	*Folio*Live
○ NAEYC: National Association for the Education of Young Children This Framework is based on the position statement of the National Association for the Education of Young Children and the National Association of Early Childhood Specialists in State Departments of Education.	*Folio*Live
○ NBPTS: National Board for Professional Teaching Standards The National Board for Professional Teaching Standards has five core propositions (NBPTS, 1999). You will find that these five propositions tie into the standards listed in the following sections. Regardless of the age or level of ability of the	*Folio*Live

Create Your Portfolio Main Page and Design

From the "My Portfolios" main page, click the title of the portfolio that you wish to work with. On the next page, click "Portfolio Settings."

To choose a design for your portfolio, select a *Folio*Live design or create a custom design (see **Creating Custom Designs** on page 28). Click "Save."

To password protect your portfolio, type a password into the "Portfolio Viewing Password" box. Viewers will need to enter this password in order to view your portfolio. Click "Save."

To add an image to your portfolio main page, go to the "My Image" section of the page. Select either "Upload Image" or "Select Existing Image" based on whether you have previously uploaded the image you want to use to *Folio*Live.

Upload Image: Select "Upload Image" and click "Browse" to select the image you want to upload from your local system. After the path to the image is visible in the box, click "Upload."

Note that there is a chart on the bottom of the screen that provides estimated upload times based on the size of the file and the connection speed of your computer to the Internet.

Select Existing Image: Select "Select Existing Image," choose the image you wish to use and click "Select Image."

The image that you selected will be listed in the box next to "My Image." Click "Save."

To add an Introductory Statement, go to the "Introductory Statement" section of the page. Type your statement directly into the text box. Click "Save."

To use HTML code within this box, select the "Text includes HTML formatting" box. HTML formatting allows you to use "tags" to modify text so that you can bold, italicize, indent, and create hotlinks to the Internet. Click "Formatting Tips," for a list of common tags and their uses.

To add your email address to your portfolio main page, check the "Show My Email Address as a Link" box. The email address that you provided during your registration process will be added. To change your email address, go to the "My Account" area.

Add an Artifact to a Portfolio

An *artifact* is any item — document or PowerPoint slide or video clip — that is added to your portfolio to demonstrate your abilities and experiences.

From the "My Portfolios" area, click on the portfolio title that you wish add artifacts to.

For Custom Portfolios, click "Create or Link to a New Artifact," and follow the directions below.

> Create or Link to an Artifact

For Framework Portfolios, first click on the placeholder you want to replace with an artifact and then follow the directions below.

My Professional Portfolio

Artifact Link	Type	Status
[?] Statement of Teaching Philosophy	Placeholder	Active
⊟ Credentials	Portfolio Section	Active
⊞ Letters of Reference	Portfolio Section	Active
↳ [?] Resume	Placeholder	Active
↳ [?] Official Transcript	Placeholder	Active
↳ [?] Record of Courses	Placeholder	Active
↳ [?] Teaching Certificate	Placeholder	Active
↳ [?] Endorsements	Placeholder	Active
⊞ Teaching-Related Experiences	Portfolio Section	Active
⊞ Community Involvement	Portfolio Section	Active
⊞ Professional Memberships & Honor Societies	Portfolio Section	Active
⊞ Extracurricular Activities	Portfolio Section	Active
☐ Select All		

[Activate]	Activate the selected artifacts.	[Reorder Portfolio] [Delete Portfolio]
[Deactivate]	Deactivate the selected artifacts.	
[Move]	Move the selected artifacts into a different porfolio section.	

To add an artifact, after clicking on "Create or Link to a New Artifact" or clicking on the Framework placeholder, click "Create a new artifact" or "Link to existing artifact(s)." Select "Link to existing artifact(s)" only if you want to link to an artifact that you uploaded or created previously in *Folio*Live.

Create or Link to an Artifact

Select "Create a new artifact" to create an artifact through *Folio***Live**.

Select "Link to existing artifact(s)" if you have uploaded the artifact in the past.

○ **Create a new artifact**

○ **Link to existing artifact(s)**

[<< Back] [Next >>]

To link to an existing artifact, after selecting "Link to an existing artifact," select the artifacts you want to add on the next screen and click "Finish."

Link to Existing Artifact(s)

Select artifact(s) that you would like to include in your portfolio. Linked artifacts can be reordered within your portfolio.

Title	Type
☐ 🄰 Resume	Text
☐ 🄰 Lesson Plan	File
☐ 🄰 Web Links	Text
☐ **Select All**	

[Finish] Link the selected items to your portfolio.

[<< Back]

To create a new artifact, after clicking "Create a new artifact," choose from the options of "Upload a file," "Add a link to a file that you have previously uploaded," "Create a new artifact using a *Folio*Live form," or "Add a link to a file on the Internet or a Web site."

Create an Artifact

Select "Upload a file" if you have not yet uploaded the artifact.

Select "Link to previously uploaded file" if you have uploaded the artifact in the past.

Select "Create a new artifact using a *FolioLive* form" to create an artifact through *FolioLive*.

Select "Add a link to a file on the Internet or a Web site" to add an artifact that is housed on the Internet.

○ **Upload a file.**

○ **Add a link to a file that you have previously uploaded.**

○ **Create a new artifact using a *FolioLive* form.**

○ **Add a link to a file on the Internet or a Web site.**

[<< Back] [Next >>]

To upload a new file, select "Upload a file" and click "Next." Enter the title. If you want the artifact to be listed under a portfolio section, select the section from the pull-down "Parent Portfolio Section" menu, or add a new section title.

To upload the file, go to the "File to Upload" area of the page. Click "Browse" to select the file you want to upload. After the path to the file is visible in the box, click "Upload." If you wish to add any of the optional information below, do so before you upload the file, or click "Edit Artifact" after it has been uploaded.

Note that there is a chart on the bottom of the screen that provides estimated upload times based on the size of the file and the connection speed of your computer to the Internet.

File to Upload (required)

[_____] (Browse...)

Please note that large files may take several minutes to upload! (see chart below)

(<< Back) (Upload)

File upload times will vary depending on your modem speed. Connections will time out after approximately 5 minutes. Use the following chart as a guideline in determining approximate upload times for your modem.

Connection speed	File size					
	100K	500K	1 MB	1.5 MB	2 MB	5 MB
14.4 Kbps	1.5 min.	X	X	X	X	X
28.8 Kbps	45 sec.	2.5 min.	X	X	X	X
33.6 Kbps	45 sec.	2.5 min.	X	X	X	X
56 Kbps	30 sec.	1.5 min.	2.5 min.	3.5 min.	X	X
128 Kbps (ISDN)	15 sec.	45 sec.	1.5 min.	2 min.	2.5 min.	X
1.5 Mbps (T1)	3 sec.	8 sec.	10 sec.	15 sec.	25 sec.	45 sec.

Note: An X indicates you should not attempt to upload a file of this size. File sizes which fall between columns might be uploadable. McGraw-Hill makes no guarantees as to the success of any upload attempt including those specified on the above table.

To make the artifact open in a new window, check the "Open artifact in a new window" box.

☐ **Open artifact in new window**

To add an introduction to the artifact, go to "Introduction" section of the page. Type your statement directly into the text box.

To use HTML code within this box, select the "Text includes HTML formatting" box. HTML formatting allows you to use "tags' to modify text so that you can bold, italicize, indent, and create hotlinks to the Internet. Click "Formatting Tips" for a list of common tags and their uses.

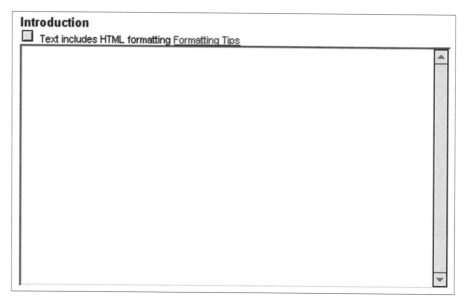

To add a reflection to the artifact, go to the "Reflection" section of the page. Type your statement directly into the text box.

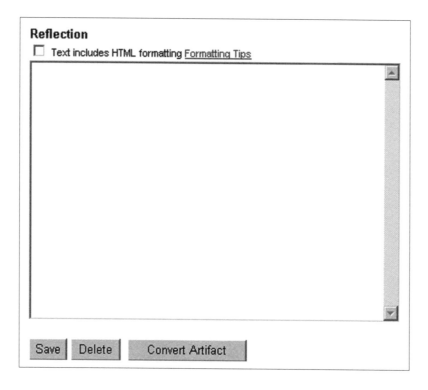

To use HTML code within this box, select the "Text includes HTML formatting" box. HTML formatting allows you to use "tags' to modify text so that you can bold, italicize, indent, and create hotlinks to the Internet. Click "Formatting Tips" for a list of common tags and their uses.

To add a file you have uploaded previously, select "Link to previously uploaded file" and click "Next." Select the file you wish to add from the listing. Click "Add." If you wish to add any of the optional information, do so before you click "Save," or click on "Edit Artifact" after it has been uploaded.

demo-s

Directories	Name	Type	Last Modified MM/DD/YYYY	Size (bytes)
demo-s	lessonplan.doc	text	07/24/2002	27,648
	image2.jpg	image	07/24/2002	50,751
	resume.rtf	file	07/24/2002	3,210
				81,609 bytes
	Add		**Total Space Available** :	**5,000,000 bytes**
			Total Space Used :	**81,609 bytes**
			Total Space Remaining :	**4,918,391 bytes**

Follow the directions on pages 20 and 21 to:

- Make the artifact open in a new window
- Add an introduction to the artifact
- Add a reflection to the artifact

To create a new artifact using a *Folio*Live form, select "Create a new artifact using a *Folio*Live form" and click "Next." Enter the title and then type the artifact text in the text box.

To use HTML code within this box, select the "Text includes HTML formatting" box. HTML formatting allows you to use "tags' to modify text so that you can bold, italicize, indent, and create hotlinks to the Internet. Click "Formatting Tips," for a list of common tags and their uses.

Add Artifact - Free-form

To add a free-form artifact, enter the Title and the text below. You may paste HTML code into the text area below. You can add the artifact to an existing or new group. Click "Add" when you are finished.

Title (required)

Text (required)

☐ Text includes HTML formatting Formatting Tips

Follow the directions on pages 20 and 21 to:

- Make the artifact open in a new window
- Add an introduction to the artifact
- Add a reflection to the artifact

To link to an artifact on the Internet, select "Add a link to a file on the Internet or a Web site" and click "Next." Type the artifact title and enter the URL.

Add Artifact - Web Link

To add an artifact located on the Internet, enter the title and URL. You can add the artifact to an existing or new group. Click "Add" when finished.

Title (required)

[   ]

URL (Web Site Address) (required)

[   ] [Test URL]

Portfolio Section   **New Portfolio Section Name**
[(none) ◆]   Create a new portfolio section: [   ] [OK]

☐ **Open artifact in new window**

Follow the directions on pages 20 and 21 to:

- Make the artifact open in a new window
- Add an introduction to the artifact
- Add a reflection to the artifact

Add a Section to a Custom Portfolio

A *section* is a collection of artifacts. For example, you may have a section entitled "Lesson Plans" under which all of your lesson plans (artifacts) are listed. From the "My Portfolios" area, click on the title of the portfolio you wish to add a section to.

To add a section, after clicking the title of the portfolio, click "Create a New Portfolio Section." Enter a title. If you would like this section to fall within another section, select this section from the pull-down "Parent Portfolio Section" menu. Click "Add New Portfolio Section."

[Create a Portfolio Section]

Add Portfolio Section

You have the option of organizing your portfolio using portfolio sections (collections of artifacts). To create a new portfolio section, enter the title below and click "Add Portfolio Section."

To place an artifact in a portfolio section, click on the artifact title on the "My Portfolio" page for the specific portfolio. A drop down menu will allow you to choose which portfolio section to place the artifact in.

Title (required)

Parent Portfolio Section
(none) ▲▼

Add Portfolio Section

Additional Information About Framework Portfolios

To add new sections to your Framework portfolio, click the portfolio title from the "My Portfolios" area and on the next page, click "Create a Portfolio Section." Enter a title. If you would like this section to fall within another section, select this section from the pull-down "Parent Portfolio Section" menu. Click "Add New Portfolio Section."

Create a Portfolio Section

Add Portfolio Section

You have the option of organizing your portfolio using portfolio sections (collections of artifacts). To create a new portfolio section, enter the title below and click "Add Portfolio Section."

To place an artifact in a portfolio section, click on the artifact title on the "My Portfolio" page for the specific portfolio. A drop down menu will allow you to choose which portfolio section to place the artifact in.

Title (required)

Parent Portfolio Section
(none) ▲▼

Add Portfolio Section

To add a new artifact (one not to be connected to a placeholder) to your Framework portfolio, click the portfolio title and on the next page, click "Create or Link to a New Artifact." Follow the directions starting on page 18 to under "Add an Artifact."

Create or Link to an Artifact

To delete a Framework section, click on the section title and on the next page, select "Delete Portfolio Section."

To delete a Framework placeholder, click on the placeholder title and on the next page, select "Delete Placeholder."

To rename a Framework section or placeholder, click on the section or place-holder title. On the next screen, enter the new title under "Title." Click "Save."

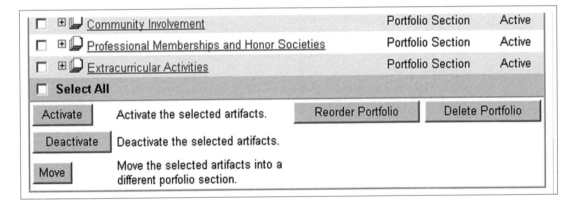

Edit Artifact Settings

To edit your artifact settings, click the "Edit Artifact" button next to the artifact title. You can then edit the title, introduction and reflection. In addition, you can move the artifact to a new portfolio section, and designate whether the artifact should open in a new window.

Edit Artifact

Manage Your Portfolio

In the "My Portfolios area," click on the title of the portfolio you are working with.

To reorder your portfolio, click "Reorder Portfolio." Place the number corresponding to where it should be placed next to the artifact. Click "Reorder." (Note: Items left blank will maintain a position relative to their current order. Precedence is given to those items with a specified index.)

To move an artifact to a Portfolio Section, select the artifact by clicking the box next to it, and click "Move." Indicate the section the artifact should be moved into, and select "Move."

To activate or deactivate artifacts, check the box next to the appropriate artifact/s and click "Activate" or "Deactivate." If you deactivate an artifact, it will not be visible on your live portfolio. It will remain in your portfolio until you delete it.

To delete an artifact, select the artifact by clicking the box next to it, and click "Delete."

To delete your portfolio, click on the portfolio title and click the "Delete Portfolio" button.

My Professional Portfolio

Artifact Link		Type	Status
☐ ? Statement of Teaching Philosophy		Placeholder	Active
☐ ⊟ Credentials		Portfolio Section	Active
☐ ⊞ Letters of Reference		Portfolio Section	Active
☐ ↳A Resume	Edit Artifact	Text	Active
☐ ↳? Official Transcript		Placeholder	Active
☐ ↳? Record of Courses		Placeholder	Active
☐ ↳? Teaching Certificate		Placeholder	Active
☐ ↳? Endorsements		Placeholder	Active
☐ ⊟ Professional Documents		Portfolio Section	Active
☐ ⊞ Teaching-Related Experiences		Portfolio Section	Active
☐ ⊞ Community Involvement		Portfolio Section	Active
☐ ⊞ Professional Memberships & Honor Societies		Portfolio Section	Active
☐ ⊞ Extracurricular Activities		Portfolio Section	Active
☐ **Select All**			

[Activate] Activate the selected artifacts.   [Reorder Portfolio] [Delete Portfolio]

[Deactivate] Deactivate the selected artifacts.

[Move] Move the selected artifacts into a different porfolio section.

CREATING CUSTOM DESIGNS

You have the option of creating a custom design for both your homepage and each of your portfolios.

If creating a custom design for your homepage, start at "My Homepage."

If creating a custom design for a portfolio, go to "My Portfolios" and click on the portfolio to which you want to add the design. Click "Portfolio Settings."

To create a custom design, click "Create/Edit My Designs." Click "Create New Design." Input a title for your design, and click "Continue."

> Create/Edit My Designs

My Designs

The "My Designs" area allows you to create your own page designs or edit an existing design. To create a new page design, click "Create New Design." To edit an existing design, click on the appropriate title in the table below.

> Create New Design

Design Title
my design

My Designs

To create a new page design, enter a title for the design and then click the "Continue" button. You will be able to customize your design by choosing page attributes. To cancel and return to the previous page, click the "Back" button.

Design Title (required)

> My Professional Design

> << Back   Continue >>

The "Specify Page Design Attributes" page allows you the option to change various elements of the page design. You can modify images such as the Header, Bullets, and the Footer, and you can modify the size, color, and style of the fonts.

Design Title: design   [Save]

[Preview Homepage]

Homepage Attributes	Current Setting
Homepage Bullet Image	Default Bullet
Homepage Header Font	36 pt, Black, bold, Arial
Homepage Title Font	14 pt, Black, bold, Arial
Homepage Text Font	12 pt, Black, Arial
Homepage Background Color	Beige

[Preview Portfolio Page]

Portfolio Attributes	Current Setting
Portfolio Header Image	Not Defined
Portfolio Bullet Image	Default Bullet
Portfolio Default Font	12 pt, Black, Arial
Portfolio Artifact Title Font	12 pt, Black, bold, Arial

To add an image (in the header or as a bullet), click on the attribute title (for example, Header Image). Choose to upload an image or to select an image that you uploaded previously. Click "Save."

To change the size of the image, enter a new width and length. Click "Save."

To add text that will appear when the mouse is moved over the image, type in the desired text in the "Alternate Text" box. Click "Save."

Add Image for Home Bullet

The "Add Image" area allows you to insert your own images on your portfolio Web pages. To specify the appearance of your page, please provide the appropriate information below. Make certain to click on the "Save" button before you exit this page.
Note: Where no changes are made, the default value for the attribute will be used.

Image Location (required)
Any photo you wish to insert here must first be saved in your "My Files" area. To go to this area, click on the link below. Once in "My Files" you can add a new image to your files or select an existing image. If you have already saved your image to "My Files" or elsewhere, you may enter the location of the image below.

[   ] [Upload Image] [Select Existing Image]

Image Width and Height (optional)
If you wish, you may specify a height and width for your image.
Note: We recommend a width of no more than 20 pixels each.

Width [ ]   **Height** [ ]

Alternate Text (optional)
You have the optional of adding alternate text, which will appear whenever the mouse is moved over the image.

[   ]

[Save]

To modify text style, click on the desired font attribute (for example, Normal Page Text Font) and select the font size, style, family and color that you would like. Click "Save."

Add Font for Home Header

The "Add Font" area allows you to choose the physical style of the text. To specifiy the appearance of your text, please make the appropriate selections below. To restore the text to the default font values, click "Restore Default."
Note: Where no changes are made, the default value for the attribute will be used as specified below.

Font Style
By default, the font style is set to 12pt., Bold, Arial, Helvetica. Choose from the selections below to change any of these settings. Click "Save" before exiting this page.
Font Size [12 ⬦]   **Text Style** ☑ **Bold** ☐ *Italic* ☐ Underline

Font Family
◉ Arial, Helvetica ○ Arial, Verdana ○ Sans Serif
○ Serif   ○ Times

To modify the background color of the page, click "Background Color." Select the color you wish to use from the pull-down menu and click "Save."

To preview your custom design, click "Preview Homepage" or "Preview Portfolio Page."

To restore the original settings, click "Restore Default."

To edit a custom design, select "Create/Edit My Designs" in the "My Homepage" area or the "Portfolio" settings area of an individual portfolio. Click on the title of the design you wish to edit. Follow the directions above under **To Create a Custom Design** starting on page 28 to make specific edits.

To delete a custom design, select "Create/Edit My Designs" in the "My Homepage" area or the "Portfolio" settings area of an individual portfolio. Click on the title of the design you wish to delete. Click "Delete Design" at the bottom of the page.

[Delete Design]

USING FRAMEWORKS AND STANDARDS

Frameworks are templates for portfolio construction. Basically, they are tables of contents with suggested artifacts. Frameworks are made up of placeholders that note where an artifact should be added. *Folio*Live Frameworks were created to provide the user with suggested portfolio tables of contents. *Note that even if you choose to use a Framework to create your portfolio, you can customize it by deleting sections and placeholders and adding new sections and artifacts.* (See "Additional Information About Framework Portfolios" on page 25.)

Using Frameworks

To create a portfolio using a Framework, see the "Create a New Portfolio" and "Add an Artifact to a Portfolio" sections in *Creating a Portfolio* starting on pages 13 and 15.

Using Standards

As standards, at both the national and state levels, play an increasing role in education, there is a growing interest in organizing portfolios around specific standards. In response, *Folio*Live offers numerous Frameworks based on standards. See *Using Standards to Construct Your Portfolio* in the online "Resources" area for more information.

To view the *Folio*Live standards-based Frameworks, go to the "My Portfolios" area. Click "Create Portfolio Using a Framework." Click the Framework title to view the placeholders within.

Preview Framework

After previewing the layout, you may click on the back button to resume your selection process for a framework.

INTASC: Interstate New Teacher Assessment and Support Consortium
The Interstate New Teacher Assessment and Support Consortium (INTASC) has identified ten standards for what beginning teachers should know. It is noteworthy to add that the National Council for Accreditation of Teacher Education (NCATE) uses the INTASC standards to evaluate teacher education programs.

Artifacts
1. Knowledge of Subject
↳ record of courses
↳ description of practicum/clinical experience
↳ research papers
↳ certificates of completion of workshops
↳ summaries of related articles
↳ bibliography of related texts
2. Standard: Learning and Human Development

To organize your portfolio around standards not yet developed into a *Folio*Live Framework, create a custom portfolio using the existing standards-based Frameworks as guides for sections and artifacts to include.

USING *MANAGE FILES*

"Manage Files" is an area that houses all of the files that you upload into your *Folio*Live account. These will consist of files you upload to become artifacts, or those used for your homepage or custom designs.

To upload a file directly into "Manage Files," go to the "Manage Files" area and click "Add a New File." Click "Browse" to select the file you want to upload from your local system. After the path to the file is listed in the box, click "Upload."

Note that there is a chart on the bottom of the screen that provides estimated upload times based on the size of the file and the connection speed of your computer to the Internet.

To create a Sub-Directory to organize your files, click "Add Sub-Directory." Enter the name for the directory and click "Create Directory."

To move a file into a directory, check the box next to the file and click "Move." Click "Tree View" and select the directory (or folder) you want to move the file into. After this is selected, click "Move."

To rename a file, check the box next to the file name and click "Rename." Enter the new name and click "Rename."

To copy a file, check the box next to the file name and click "Copy." Click "Tree View" and indicate where you want the file copied. Click "Copy."

To delete a file, check the box next to the file and click "Delete."

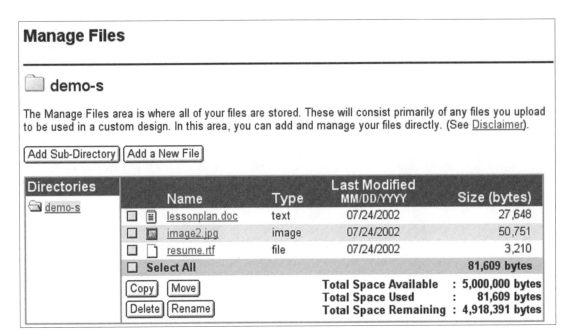

Note: For a file to become an artifact, it must be uploaded into a portfolio or to "Manage Artifacts" as an artifact.

USING *MANAGE ARTIFACTS*

The "Manage Artifacts" area houses all of your artifacts. An *artifact* is any item — image or document or PowerPoint slide or video clip — that is added to your portfolio to demonstrate your abilities and experiences. When you upload a new artifact, it is stored here. When you create a new artifact using a *Folio*Live form, it is housed here. You will need to use "Manage Artifacts" only if you want to add an artifact directly to this area, or if you want to manage the artifacts in the area. When you add an artifact to a portfolio using "Link to previously uploaded artifact," you will be linked to "Manage Artifacts" area to select the artifact.

To add an artifact directly to "Manage Artifacts," go to the "Manage Artifacts" area and click "Add New Artifact." Your options for adding a new artifact include (see "Add an Artifact to a Portfolio" on page 19:

1. "Upload a new file"
2. "Link to previously uploaded file"
3. "Create a new artifact using a *Folio*Live form"
4. "Add a link to a file on the Internet or a Web site"

To edit your artifact, its introduction, reflection, or features, go to the "Manage Artifacts" area and click on the artifact title. Make changes and click "Save." You can also make these revisions in the "My Portfolios" area by clicking the "Edit Artifact" button next to the artifact name.

To convert your artifact into another type of artifact, click "Convert." Select the type of artifact you would like it converted into.

To reorder your artifacts, click "Reorder Artifacts" and input a number in the space next to the artifact to indicate its new position. Click "Reorder."

To activate or deactivate an artifact, select the artifact and click "Activate" or "Deactivate."

Manage Artifacts

This area houses all of your artifacts. *Folio***Live** links directly to this area from the "My Portfolios" area to add artifacts to your portfolios or link them to placeholders.

This area can be used to add, edit, and manage your artifacts directly.

[Add a New Artifact] [Reorder Artifacts]

	Title	Type	Status
☐	🄰 Resume	Text	Active
☐	🄰 Lesson Plan	File	Active
☐	🄰 Web Links	Text	Active
☐	**Select All**		

[Activate]   Activate the selected artifacts in all of your portfolios.

[Deactivate] Deactivate the selected artifacts in all of your portfolios.

JOINING A COURSE

The "Join a Course" area allows you to link your portfolio to your instructor's course Web site. When you join an instructor's course, you will have access to any Frameworks that your instructor creates. Additionally, your instructor will be able to provide direct feedback on your portfolio and artifacts. Your instructor's *Folio*Live Course Web site will include a link to your homepage and portfolios.

To Join a Course, click "Join a Course" on the left-hand menu. Enter the URL for your instructor's Homepage or Course Web site in the box at the bottom of the page. Click "Continue." Select the specific course you want to join, and click "Join."

To view the courses you have joined, go to the "Join a Course" area.

To detach yourself from a course, go to the "Join a Course" area, select the course you want to detach from, and click "Detach."

Join A Course

If you are using *Folio*Live in conjunction with a course, the "Join a Course" feature allows you to link your homepage to your instructor?s *Folio*Live course Web site.

To "Join a Course," your instructor must provide you with his/her *Folio*Live course Web site URL(and possibly a password).

You are currently registered for the for the following courses:

Course Title	Instructor	Status in Course
☐ EDU 101 Intro to Education	Professor Smith	Active
☐ **Select All**		

[Detach] Detach from the selected course(s).

To join a course, enter your instructor's *Folio*Live Web site address and click "Continue."
Instructor's *Folio*Live URL (required)

`http://demo-i.foliolive.net`

[Continue >>]

Note: If you have password protected your homepage or portfolio, you will need to give your instructor the password so that he or she may access it. Alternatively, you can remove the password protection.

DOWNLOADING YOUR PORTFOLIO

Your *Folio*Live homepage and electronic portfolios are housed on the McGraw-Hill server. You have the option of downloading your portfolios. By downloading your portfolios, you can store them on your local system and/or burn them onto a CD-Rom.

To download your portfolios to your local system, go to the "Download Portfolio" area. Click "Download Portfolio." Your portfolio will be saved to your local system as a ZIP file. In order to open the ZIP file, you will need to have the WinZip program. If you do not already have WinZip installed, you can access it for free (for 30 days) at www.winzip.com.

After your portfolio has been downloaded to your local system, "right-click" on the file and choose to "Extract to Folder." You will then need to point your system to where you want to save the file. Once the file has been extracted, your portfolios will be in individual folders. The folders will have the same structure as your portfolios did in *Folio*Live.

Download Portfolio

Click on "Download Portfolio Now" button to attempt your download. *Folio***Live** has placed limits on the number of portfolios that can be downloaded at any one time. If the system is already processing the maximum number of portfolio downloads, you will have to try again. The Browse feature will allow you to indicate where you would like to save the file.

Note: Your file will be saved as a ZIP file. This file will contain all of the files and directories inside the desired portfolio. In order to open the ZIP file and save the files in the exact way that they are structured on the *Folio***Live** server, follow these important instructions.

You MUST have the WinZip program to open the ZIP file. If you do not have this program it can be downloaded for free by simply visiting the WinZip Web site at http://www.winzip.com.

After the ZIP file has been saved to your local drive, go to that file and, using your mouse, RIGHT CLICK on the ZIP file. Scroll down to the "Extract folder to C:/..." option. Your files will automatically save into folders that match those in the *Folio***Live** directory.

[Download Porfolio]

MANAGING YOUR *FOLIO*LIVE ACCOUNT

The "My Account" area summarizes your account information. In this area you can find out:

- When your *Folio*Live account will expire
- How much server space you have used and have left

In addition, you can edit your name, email address, phone number, and fax number; as well as change your account log-in password and Web site URL, and view when your account expires. Click "Save" after making any changes.

Upon registering for *Folio*Live, you will have access to the product for one year. You can renew access in one-year increments. You will receive notification through your *Folio*Live account of when your access is ending. Renewal instructions will be provided.

My Account

This page allows you to modify your account information.

Product   **Expiration Date**
FolioLive for Education   Does not expire

Drivespace

In use: 81,609 bytes
Free: 4,918,391 bytes
Limit: 5,000,000 bytes

[Change Your Log-in Password]

First Name (required)
Nancy

Last Name (required)
Jones

E-mail (required)
njones@college.edu

GETTING HELP

For technical help, contact McGraw-Hill Software Support at 1-800-331-5094 or techsup@mcgraw-hill.com; or visit the Help Desk at www.mhhe.com/helpdesk. The Help Desk is open from 8:00am to 5:30pmCST.

Developing and Maintaining Your Electronic Portfolio

You may have purchased *Folio*Live because it was assigned by one of your instructors. Or, you may have purchased *Folio*Live independently to aid you in the creation of your electronic portfolio. In either case, you have taken an important first step in the development of your electronic portfolio — you have started it. We strongly recommend that your electronic portfolio be something that grows with you, rather than something you ever "finish."

The Professional Portfolio as a Concept[*]

In their 1998 manual from the University of Maryland, *Developing a Professional Teaching Portfolio, A Guide for Educators* (1998), Constantino and DeLorenzo explore the development and use of portfolios. The importance of portfolios is outlined in the text using the reasons listed below. As you can see from these eight attributes, creating your own portfolio is a worthwhile, necessary endeavor.

- Portfolios facilitate the development of reflective thinking.
- Portfolios present a holistic view of your achievements.
- Portfolios provide an ongoing record of your accomplishments.
- Portfolios place the responsibility on you to develop and plan for your goals.
- Portfolios correlate with national and state initiatives toward performance-based assessment.
- Portfolios may be used to document and validate teaching accomplishments.
- Portfolios may be used to assess preservice and inservice teacher performances.
- Portfolios enhance job searches and interview processes.

Types of Portfolios[*]

The term "portfolio" is one of the most commonly used buzzwords in the education profession today. Some of the people most likely to use portfolios are under-

[*] Based on Rieman, Patricia. *Teaching Portfolios: Presenting Your Professional Best.* New York: McGraw-Hill, 2000.

graduate education majors, student teachers, new teachers, tenured teachers, and higher education faculty.

- Professional portfolios are maintained by undergraduate college students to document skills and experiences.
- Student teachers update their portfolios to prepare them for those crucial first interviews.
- New teachers keep all their lesson plans, evaluations, and communication documents in portfolios to show their organization, growth, and readiness for tenure.
- Tenured teachers wishing to become nationally certified "master teachers" will include artifacts of post-graduate work accomplished, diversity of students taught, peer evaluations, letters of recommendation by parents and students, and copies of outstanding lesson plans and samples of student work following those plans.
- Finally, university-level educators will wish to document their achievements, such as dissertations, publications, awards, speaking engagements, evaluations, and advanced coursework as they pursue full professorships.

As you can see, portfolio maintenance is developmental and on-going—one may even consider it a major component of being a professional educator.

GLOSSARY

Artifact: Any item included in a portfolio used as tangible evidence of ability or accomplishment.

Custom Portfolio: In *Folio*Live, a portfolio that the user creates from scratch.

Electronic Portfolio: A portfolio that consists of electronic files – whether online, on a CD-ROM, or a local network.

Framework: In *Folio*Live, a portfolio table of contents (or outline) that includes suggestions for artifacts. It is a template for creating a portfolio by linking actual artifacts to the placeholders for suggested artifacts. A Framework consists of a group of placeholders.

Framework Portfolio: In *Folio*Live, a portfolio that the user creates based on a Framework.

Placeholder: In *Folio*Live, indicates where an artifact should be placed. A group of placeholders is a Framework.

Portfolio: A purposeful collection of your best teaching efforts.

Section: In *Folio*Live, a group of artifacts.

Sub-Directory: In *Folio*Live, a group of files in *Manage Files*.

INDEX

Account, *see also* My Account, 9
Additional, *8*
Alternate Text, 30
Artifact, 16, 45
   activate, 27, 37–38
   add through *Manage Artifacts,* 37–38
   add to custom portfolio, 16, 18–26
   add to Framework portfolio, 17, 18–26
   deactivate, 27, 37–38
   delete, 27, 37–38
   introduction, 21–22, 23, 24
   open in new window, 20, 22, 23, 24
   reflection, 21–22, 23, 24
   reorder, 27, 37–38
Authoring, 6

Benefits to user, 1, 3

Contact information, 41
Custom portfolio, *see also* Portfolio, 13, 45
   artifact, add, 16, 18–26
   delete, 27
   section, add, 24–25

Design
   custom, 15, 28–31
   edit, 31
   *Folio*Live provided, 10, 15
   homepage, 10
   image, 29
   My Designs, 10, 28
   portfolio, 15
   preview, 31
Download portfolio, 40

Electronic portfolio, *see also* Portfolio, 2
   employers, and 2
   why use, 1–2
Email Address
   homepage, 12
   My Account, 41
   portfolio, 16

Framework, 32, 45
   *Folio*Live Frameworks, 32
   preview, 33
   use, 14, 17
Framework portfolio, *see also* Portfolio, 14, 45
   add artifact, 17, 18–26
   *Folio*Live provided Frameworks, 33
   placeholders, 45
   add section, 25

Help, 8, 42
Help Desk, 8, 42
Homepage, 10–12
   activate, 12
   create, 10–12
   deactivate, 12
   design, 10
   email address, 12
   image, 10–11
     select existing image, 11
     upload image, 11
   Introductory Statement, 11
     HTML, 11
   password protect, 12
HTML,
   artifact, 23

introduction, 20
introductory statement, 11, 15
reflection, 22

Image, 10–11
  bullet, add to, 29
   add alternate text, 30
   change size, 29
  footer, add to, 29
   add alternate text, 30
   change size, 29
  header, add to, 29
   add alternate text, 30
   change size, 29
  homepage, add to, 10
  portfolio, add to, 15
  select existing image, 10, 15
  upload image, 10, 15
Introduction
  artifact, add to, 12–22, 23, 24
  HTML, 20
Introductory Statement, 11, 15
  homepage, 11
  HTML, 11, 15
  portfolio, 15

Join a Course, 7, 39
  detach from course, 39
  view courses joined to, 39

Logging-in, 9
Log Out, 8

Manage Artifacts, 7, 37–38
  activate artifact, 37–38
  add artifact, 37–38
  convert artifact, 37–38
  deactivate artifact, 37–38
  edit artifact, 37–38
  reorder artifact, 37–38
Manage Files, 7, 35–36
  copy file, 35–36
  move file, 35–36
  rename file, 35–36
  sub-directory, 35–36, 45

  upload file, 35–36
My Account, 7, 41
  contact information, 41
  email address, 41
  expiration date, 41
  renewal, 9
  server space, 41
  URL, 41
My Homepage, 6
My Portfolios, 7

Parent portfolio section
  custom portfolio, 24
  framework portfolio, 25
Password protection
  homepage, 12
  instructors, and, 39
  portfolio, 15
Placeholder, 17, 45
Portfolio, *see also* Electronic Portfolio, 1–2,
   43–44, 45
  artifact, 45
   add to custom, 16, 18–26
   add to Framework, 17, 18–26
   delete, 27
   move, 27
   reorder, 27
  create new, 13–27
  Custom portfolio, *see also* Custom
   Portfolio, 13, 45
  design, 15
  download, 40
  electronic, 15
  email address, 16
  employers, and, 2
  *Folio*Live provided Frameworks, 32–33
  Framework portfolio, *see also* Framework
   Portfolio, 14, 45
  image, add, 15
  Introductory Statement, 15
  manage, 27
  password protect, 15
  reorder, 27
  section, add to custom, 24–25
  section, add to Framework, 25

settings, 26
   edit, 26
Placeholders, 45

Reflection, 21–22
   artifact, add to, 21
   HTML, 22
Renew Access, 9
Reorder, 27
Resources, 7

Section, 45
   custom portfolio, add, 24–25
   delete, 24–25
   edit, 24–25
   framework portfolio, add, 25

move, 25
   parent portfolio section, 24–25
   reorder, 27
Server Space, 41
Standards, 32
   standards-based portfolio, 33
   *Using Standards to Construct Your
     Portfolio,* 32
Sub-directory, 35–36, 45
Start Here, 6

Text style, 30–31

URL, 10, 41
Utility, 7